R

X

for Joy...
365 GRATITUDE
AFFIRMATIONS

From Joan to my
dear sister Myrtle —

Many blessings,
Clancy

R X *for Joy…* 365 GRATITUDE AFFIRMATIONS

Take one daily

Dr. Clancy Blakemore

BALBOA.
PRESS

A DIVISION OF HAY HOUSE

Rx for Joy...365 GRATITUDE AFFIRMATIONS
Take one daily

ISBN: 978-1-4525-5890-5 (sc)
ISBN: 978-1-4525-5891-2 (e)

Balboa Press books may be ordered through booksellers or by contacting:

Balboa Press
A Division of Hay House
1663 Liberty Drive
Bloomington, IN 47403
www.balboapress.com
1-(877) 407-4847

Printed in the United States of America

Balboa Press rev. date: 9/27/2012

To my loving husband Richard

In everything give thanks. An attitude of gratitude is most salutary, and bespeaks the realization that we are now in heaven…

We have to become quiet and, in the solitude of our own thought, discover for ourselves what it is we actually believe; and then proceed to put that faith into creative action through patterns of thinking built around that faith…

We do not change all of the patterns of our thought in a moment. Rather, it takes place little by little, until gradually the old thought patterns become transformed into new ones…the operation of which we do not see but the manifestation of which we do experience…

Ernest Holmes

Now *faith* is the substance of things hoped for…
it is the evidence of things not seen.

Hebrews 11:1

Therefore I say to you, anything you pray for and *ask, believe*
that you will receive it, and it will be done for you.

Mark 11:24

Trust in the Lord;
and *he shall give you* the desires of your heart.

Psalms 37:4

…the worthy person is grateful and mindful of benefits done to him.
This gratitude, this mindfulness, is congenial to the best people.

Buddhism

One upon whom we bestow kindness
But will not express gratitude,
Is worse than a robber
Who carries away our belongings.

African Traditional Religious

Contents

Forward ———————————

Dr. Ernest Holmes writes, "Repeating an affirmation is leading the mind to that state of consciousness where it accepts that which it wishes to believe." If our actions or thoughts vary from what we say we believe, making affirmations daily will be the spiritual detectors indicating where we are off course. It is then we correct our thinking and actions, and move easily within God to our heart's desire.

Dr. Clancy Blakemore has given us a wonderful gift in *Rx for Joy; 365 GRATITUDE AFFIRMATIONS*. She is uniquely qualified to pen such a treasure given that she represents the qualities of gratitude and boundless joy as anyone who has been privileged to know her would gladly affirm. Follow this prescription and *live* your life instead of a mere joyless meager existence.

Rev. Dr. Lloyd George Tupper

Acknowledgments

I am grateful for my dear husband Richard, who was always willing to say "Yes" to my requests for reading the most recent version of the book and consistently cheers me on.

I am grateful for my family and friends who accept everything I write, with enthusiasm, joy and encouragement.

I am grateful that over 30 years ago a dear friend, Karen McKee, invited me to visit the Huntington Beach Church of Religious Science. Even though I "didn't do church," I found myself returning Sunday after Sunday for inspiration, and I experienced a community of bright, caring people. My feeling was, "I have come home!"

I am grateful that the Senior Minister, Dr. Peggy Basset presented the spiritual message of unity and love, with delightful grace, humor and vitality. Classes followed and soon I would express: "This is a spiritual philosophy for successful everyday living, and it works for me!" Years later, Dr. Peggy became my mentor through seminary and hired me into my first position as a minister.

I am grateful that so many friends were willing to proof and offer support during the writing process: Joan Hyde and Billie Shawl for their creative input and loving encouragement. David Ziessler and Ann Helgerman offered their editorial suggestions and proofreading. Nancy Brunson "wiggled her nose" and created computer clarity and much assistance.

I am grateful that our grandson Tyler Pagan shared his awesome talent with the sketch that appears throughout the book. Thanks to Larry Ficken, who is following his bliss and offered his lovely cover photography.

This book project would certainly echo, "It takes a village!"

Change Your Thinking, Your Feelings and Transform your Experience… One Gratitude Affirmation a Day!

A delightful song from "The Sound of Music" reminds us to "Begin at the very beginning, that's a very good place to start…"

Each year I create something different as a gift for our family. After writing 365 affirmations of gratitude, I shared the booklet with some friends. It was suggested that others might like to have a book focused on gratitude, as there are so many benefits experienced through acknowledging the blessings in our lives every single day. Some of the benefits people feel are, less stress, more balance and energy, a greater sense of joy in life. And so you have at hand *Rx for Joy* to support the transformation of your life experiences.

There are 52 weeks of spiritual Truth statements to remind you of your innate magnificence, as well the tool of 365 powerful daily affirmations of gratitude. You may already have proven to yourself that; "Where my attention goes, my energy flows, and the result shows." Putting your attention on everything for which you are grateful every day, you are consciously taking charge of the tendency of your thoughts and feelings. This is a sacred spiritual practice as you acknowledge your worth, and your life being lived within God's Presence. Your results *will* show how affirmations are making a positive difference in your life!

- Start with the date you begin reading the book or just start wherever you wish. It seems that often the affirmation read is *the one* for that day.
- Read the weekly reminder and the gratitude affirmation for the date.
- Consider how this affirmation may apply to your life.
- Journal or take notes, as is appropriate to your own style of contemplation.
- Have a dialogue with someone about your increasing feelings of gratitude, joy and balance. This will enrich your experience. A friend said, "Reading the daily affirmations, I'm surprised how many different things I'm really grateful for!"

- Experiment creating your own gratitude affirmations. If you have not done this, below is a simple, proven process for writing them. Writing often helps to clarify your thinking and feeling. Looking back at what you have written will assist you to realize your successes and encourage you to persist and move beyond any previously perceived limitations.

A "P-elicious" Recipe for Empowering Affirmations
(Note that each ingredient and process begins with the letter "P" creating a "P-elicious"- a delicious result.)
- **P**reparation: Quiet time to get in touch with your good desires and the highest truth of your being.
- **P**urpose: A word or short phrase that states what good you want to experience more of in your life.

Recipe Ingredients:
- **P**ersonal: I, me, my, or any first person pronoun.
- **P**resent tense: "am" and "now" type verbs. Words like "tomorrow", "sometime" or "I *will*", put off your good. Remember that "tomorrow" never comes, and the "present" is a gift from God.
- **P**owerful words: Word images that stimulate your feelings of joy and success.
- **P**ositive: Only affirm what you *want* rather than what you *don't want*, realizing that your higher power within only wants what is good for you. Recognize that there is a power for good, God, and you can align with that power.

When you have written a simple gratitude affirmation, then:
- **P**ractice: It often takes many repetitions of your consciously chosen empowering thoughts to act as an antidote to your "up-until-now" more disempowering thinking. You probably have noticed that most of the messages from the world-at-large are usually negative in nature. You may find it helpful to place your written affirmations around your work area, your home and other places, to visually remind you of your innate power to create your own experience.
- **P**ersevere: Re-write your affirmations until they are easy to remember and use, to keep you on the road of empowerment.

And "keep on keeping on" as you remember the principle of cause and effect: "Where my attention goes, my energy flows, and the result shows."

Here is an example of an affirmation that contains all of the "**P**-elicious" ingredients: *I am grateful I live and move within the vitality of God. Every cell in my body is vibrating with joy, energy and ease!*

Your mind may chatter, "Yeh, but you don't understand how that can't work! You're just kidding yourself. You don't know *my* terrible story and what has happened to me in life!"

Tomato seeds do not look like tomatoes, and yet when you plant them you can be assured you will harvest tomatoes and not onions. Remember; your gratitude affirmations are planting your desired Truth-thought seeds and you will harvest a richer life.

The way it works is this: God/Infinite Spirit/your higher power/ Love/Limitless Potential/Creator/Source, is always responding with a "Yes!" It provides the power to activate that which is the tendency of your thinking and feelings. It is a principle, and it truly *is* done unto you *as* you believe. Just as mathematics does not determine how you use it, it just works!

Frantic Focus + *Fear* Feelings = *Freakin'* Results.
Fantastic Focus + *Faith* Feelings = *Fabulous* Results.

An empowering spiritual principle equation might read:
Fantastic Gratitude Focus + *Faith* Feelings =
Fabulous Results of joy, balance, harmony,
and a deepening sense of well-being!

Read and repeat daily gratitude affirmations. Write your own empowering affirmations that are filled with enthusiasm, optimism and confidence. Claim your good desires that harm no one, and your highest ultimate outcome is assured.

We have many thousands of thoughts each day! How many of these thoughts are those that you are consciously choosing as gratitude, empowering and enriching thoughts? How many of these thoughts are simply repetitions of your old stories from yesterday?

If this is your first day (or the last day) in this body-life, what do you want to be creating? More love? More joy and fun? Greater emotional balance? Improved mental and physical health? More compassion and abundant living from your heart being more open and receptive? A deeper sense of peace and harmony? Expressing gratitude in varied ways has been proven to assist in creating these experiences.

May you pay attention, guide the tendency of your thoughts and feelings, knowing you do attract that to which you are paying your "golden coin of attention."

Focus your intention and your attention. Realize that there can only be the Source, the presence and power called by many names. Connect to this very essence of being and rejoice that you are living *within* this higher power, this one mind, the one heart of joy and peace.

Reviewing your gratitude affirmations just before going to sleep impresses your subconscious mind, so during sleep the thought-feeling seeds you have been planting are growing in vital soil. You are taking charge of your life, opening to new limitless possibilities and creating a new habit pattern. You are transforming your life, one gratitude affirmation at a time!

May your blessings greatly increase, as you acknowledge and celebrate the many gifts you have already been given by a Loving God, the Creative Source. It is your natural birthright and you are worth it!

January

I am grateful as I remember that in *this moment, all is well*...Whatever my challenges, my new "opportunities for growth," my fresh beginnings in a relationship, an increasing acceptance of my expanding and limitless abundance, good, love and joy, God is already delivering the gifts! As this is true about me, it is also the ultimate Truth for every one of Spirit's creations.

In *this moment, all is well*...So it is with an open heart, with joyful expectancy, assurance, and a peacefully balanced mind that I remember to return again and again to *this moment*...

My Personal Gratitude Affirmations

Day 1

I am grateful that regardless of the circumstances or appearances, God is present in my life now! What a feeling of joy to know this!

Day 2

I am grateful for the opportunities in *this day*, and I'm delighted to say, "I care about you and want the best for you!"

Day 3

I am grateful that with each breath I take I can release old ideas I no longer need and I inhale more love, grace and vitality. I am experiencing greater calm and peace right now.

Day 4

I am grateful for my senses that stimulate my mind with delightful images of energy. I feel enthusiastic!

Day 5

I am grateful for increasing awareness of the variety of ways I may use my creativity, and I feel inspired.

Day 6

I am grateful that I have many ways to communicate with people I love and care about, and I feel a growing freedom in my relationships.

Day 7

I am grateful that as I release the past I am able to see new vistas of increasing abundance. I feel more youthful and adventurous.

January

I am grateful and joyful as I acknowledge the cleansing, healing, freeing power of laughing with friends…for support and beauty that is magnified and multiplied as it is shared with the world…for knowing that God is always present, within, around and through me and through everyone, everywhere.

My Personal Gratitude Affirmations

_____
_____
_____
_____
_____
_____
_____
_____
_____
_____
_____
_____
_____
_____
_____
_____
_____
_____
_____
_____
_____
_____
_____
_____
_____
_____
_____
_____
_____

Day 8

I am grateful that I can rejoice in limitless possibilities. I hear the Infinite calling me to enjoy all the gifts that are mine, for my pleasure and expression. I feel worthy of these gifts.

Day 9

I am grateful that as I anticipate only goodness from each activity and encounter, only a feeling of increased balance comes to me.

Day 10

I am grateful that the "business" of my life is empowered and enriched by unusual opportunities. I feel richer, now!

Day 11

I am grateful that my life is full and overflowing with vitality which moves through my mind and body. I am feeling constantly more empowered.

Day 12

I am grateful I can name my good and claim it for myself and my friends, with greatly increasing feelings of kinship and oneness.

Day 13

I am grateful that every step I take furthers my understanding and deepens my awareness that my gifts come from many sources. God is extravagantly showering me with these blessings!

Day 14

I am grateful that I live in an unlimited environment and my life is delightfully enriched.

January

I am grateful I am making a new commitment to myself to take the time for renewal and "re-creation". I breathe deeply knowing that I can facilitate my own retreat, in *this* moment of now, right where I am. Whatever choice I make from a connection with my inner being is the right choice for me. I am thankful I understand this.

My Personal Gratitude Affirmations

_____
_____
_____
_____
_____
_____
_____
_____
_____
_____
_____
_____
_____
_____
_____
_____
_____
_____
_____
_____
_____
_____
_____
_____
_____
_____
_____

Day 15

I am grateful that my finances are increasingly abundant and in harmony with all of my financial agreements. I feel more secure each and every day.

Day 16

I am grateful that I have the opportunity today to forgive someone. Doing so I know I too am forgiven. I feel the cycle of love returning to me.

Day 17

I am grateful that a healing spirit resides in every cell of my being and with this awareness I am feeling healthy, happy, and alive!

Day 18

I am grateful that my joy is enthusiastically expressed in the many ways I choose to act each day. I feel my "joy-spotlight" at work!

Day 19

I am grateful that God-love abounds in, around and through me and I can feel it moving me to new, exciting heights of abundant joy.

Day 20

I am grateful that my life is a banquet of challenges, choices and dividends. I feel loving and I love life!

Day 21

I am grateful for the beauty of nature that hides and reveals itself in little bursts of color, form and action that makes my life fascinating. These gifts of the Infinite tell me I am loved.

January

I am grateful I am on an adventure of discovery, and I am moving forward with enthusiasm, joy, and genuine expectancy of the highest and best outcome. I am identifying my skills, talents, creativity and joy that I am bringing to this next step in my life. I am being drawn to a specific situation, and there are no obstacles to my discovery. Supportive people and exciting circumstances are assisting me along this path.

My Personal Gratitude Affirmations

_____
_____
_____
_____
_____
_____
_____
_____
_____
_____
_____
_____
_____
_____
_____
_____
_____
_____
_____
_____
_____
_____
_____
_____
_____
_____
_____
_____

Day 22

I am grateful for the awareness that I am valuable, loving and creative. I can feel and experience these wonderful qualities.

Day 23

I am grateful that as I greet this day with love and extend it to each person that I see I feel the love coming back to me! "GOGI!" Good out, good in!

Day 24

I am grateful that there are many ways to experience, celebrate and worship God, and I feel in awe. My relationship with the Infinite is freeing and feels intimate!

Day 25

I am grateful for the Spirit of God-love expressing through me as love. As I dance "Love's Dance" with Spirit, goodness bursts forth all around me.

Day 26

I am grateful for each person I meet as I go through my day and I share the warmth of my heart with a smile. I feel the warmth of reflected light.

Day 27

I am grateful that my prosperity is like a tsunami that overflows my shores. I can hardly contain the flood. I am awash in God's supply.

Day 28

I am grateful for the many gifts in my life and my gifts keep growing. I feel affluent!

January

I am grateful there are a myriad of family members, friends and resources to cheer me on my pathway. My new intentions and commitments are empowered by the encouragement, the "big heart", offered to me without judgment or attachment. This is a tremendous daily blessing.

My Personal Gratitude Affirmations

Day 29

I am grateful that I can let go of any self-imposed limits and reach for new heights of possible dreams. As I do so, those dreams actually become a part of my new experience. Sometimes I feel amused and smile at the out-picturing I imagine.

Day 30

I am grateful that my life is harmonious and joyous! This is heaven and I feel free, loved and so thankful for the life I am creating with my consciousness that is connected with God-source.

Day 31

I am grateful for the responsiveness of Spirit's energy as I calmly seek wisdom and guidance. I am filled by this act and cannot help but share Spirit's gifts with those I touch. Once again I learn that I cannot out-give the Infinite.

February

I am grateful my journey of awakening is a path of healing, revealing the truth of my wholeness. This is my path of fulfillment. This is a journey that allows me to re-tune my eyes and ears to the present moment, and acknowledge my strengths. From this acceptance I can more easily move from a place of *fear* to a place of *faith* and assurance.

My Personal Gratitude Affirmations

Day 1

I am grateful that I can move beyond any prior limited thinking and begin to experience a rich, zesty, adventurous life that I love. I am excited!

Day 2

I am grateful for the beauty that surrounds me and I feel energized with love and light.

Day 3

I am grateful that today with great confidence I can step through my challenges, to meet my successes and rewards, with great feelings of accomplishment. Wow! Does that feel good!

Day 4

I am grateful that today I am joyously reaching out to catch the golden ring on the merry-go-round of life. Each revolution is fresh and new and I feel alert and alive, like a child again.

Day 5

I am grateful that today is a gentle day that refreshes my mind, body and spirit. I feel serene, fresh and clear.

Day 6

I am grateful that I can look beyond the clouds of doubt and confusion, knowing that infinite wisdom and guidance is always available. Now, feeling poised, I see the truth of the sunlit day and the starry night.

Day 7

I am grateful that as I feel at-one with God, troubling questions are being answered. As I trust this guidance and wisdom I meet with the rewards of a maturing faith. God never fails.

February

I am grateful to understand that enthusiasm means God-inspired, possessed or filled with God's light and power. I have a unique way of expressing enthusiasm in my life. As I look around, I notice people who appear enthusiastic and inspired. Enthusiastic people express the love which they feel. This is a new day, a day for me to step out into life and *be* the fully enthusiastic expression of Spirit that I *am*. As I reach out to others, they too will feel more love, more joy, and more God-inspired enthusiasm!

My Personal Gratitude Affirmations

Day 8

I am grateful for my feelings that allow me to touch another's life with compassion. Doing so, I realize more fully my unique purpose.

Day 9

I am grateful that I can bask in the gentle rhythm and balancing flow of life's cycles of change.

Day 10

I am grateful that many empowering idea seeds are planted today and I feel wonderful as I reap the greater harvest of good.

Day 11

I am grateful that every part of my physical body is vitally energized from the powerhouse of Life and I easily live my life with energy to spare.

Day 12

I am grateful that I have a deep appreciation for the common-day miracles which move me forward with excitement, faith and an awareness of the amazing unfolding of my life.

Day 13

I am grateful that limitless opportunities for self expression are mine. I reflect the creative intention of the Creator and I am delighted as I explore the infinite possibilities before me.

Day 14

I am grateful and celebrate anew, my ability to move freely, and dance through life light-heartedly. I feel the vitality and freedom that God constantly supplies.

February

I am grateful I am now, and always have been, complete and whole. I honor the child within myself that helped me to survive, and I lovingly embrace it. At the same time, I forgive myself for any "unskilled behavior" I may have been using in today's world. From the place of loving myself just as I am and just as I have been, I tap the richness of the love that is in me. That realization begins to bless my life and it is returned to me with greatly increasing blessings.

My Personal Gratitude Affirmations

Day 15

I am grateful that I can recognize in each moment the empowerment of silent prayer. In these moments I am so aware of my oneness with the Infinite and I am forever changed.

Day 16

I am grateful that my senses bring many varied stories to my mind and I rejoice in the feelings they stimulate. In this way the past becomes now as time stands still.

Day 17

I am grateful for life's opportunities for growth, which may sometimes be challenging. I am rewarded as I trust the goodness of God.

Day 18

I am grateful that today I am discovering more people with exploring minds with whom to share my adventures. I feel enriched and full.

Day 19

I am grateful that today I am creating a deeper commitment to my authentic self and to sharing that self with others. I feel guided and reassured by God-wisdom and love.

Day 20

I am grateful that I can see the potential of others and encourage them to reach their highest good. I feel the richness they bring to my life.

Day 21

I am grateful that I have an open and giving heart. I recognize that it is truly blessed to offer a helping hand without an expectation of reward. In the giving I receive blessings, inspiration and satisfaction.

February

I am grateful I affirm and know the truth about myself. I am Spiritual essence in human form, and must therefore be whole and perfect, an expression of love, joy, acceptance and peace. As a creation of God, I cannot be otherwise, and any thought or idea to the contrary is false. God-love is more powerful than anything. Only love can triumph in my relationships, beginning with the one I see when I look in the mirror. Acceptance as simple as that expressed by a pet is a divine reminder of ever-present love. I know too that I am blessed as I move into this fresh heart-centered understanding about everyone.

This is a beautiful time of year to expand awareness of my blessings, and from love, be happy with myself, my family and friends, with or without any changes!

My Personal Gratitude Affirmations

Day 22

I am grateful that love is everywhere and I am open to receive and feel it.

Day 23

I am grateful for my good health. I *believe* it therefore I *experience* it in feeling, thought and action. My good health is given to me as I believe. In essence it is a gift to me!

Day 24

I am grateful that as I release all of my doubts, I am forging on toward the fulfillment of my dreams. I have an increasing sense of confidence, faith and a growing feeling of accomplishment.

Day 25

I am grateful for the richness and the feeling of abundance which permeates my life. These qualities are like a warm light that illuminates my daily life.

Day 26

I am grateful that even as I goof, I learn and get going forward again. I feel a great wonder at life.

Day 27

I am grateful that I know the consequences of life are bad or good only in the eyes of those who judge them that way. To avoid such consequences I am releasing my judgments and already I am feeling freer.

Day 28

I am grateful that I love life and I live life fully! I am feeling more youthful with the passing of each day.

March

I am grateful I know that I have within myself all of the limitless potential to uniquely respond to life. I am not limited in any way by my heritage or another's preconceptions. I am developing my talents which send me moving confidently out into the world. I am composing my own music, speaking my own magical prose. I am filled with the vital poetry of life. I have a rich zest for boundless, harmonious living. I am fully expressing every day in every way.

My Personal Gratitude Affirmations

_____
_____
_____
_____
_____
_____
_____
_____
_____
_____
_____
_____
_____
_____
_____
_____
_____
_____

Day 1

I am grateful that Love is everywhere, and I revel in all the love that surrounds me.

Day 2

I am grateful that I am releasing unkind thoughts, and am re-looking with love at those whom I may have judged in the past. I feel wiser and freer in the process.

Day 3

I am grateful that I can use confusion and indecision like friendly teachers that re-direct my thoughts and intentions toward empowering clarity and wise decisions.

Day 4

I am grateful that I feel increasingly tranquil and peaceful as I am going through this day.

Day 5

I am grateful to those who share their lessons of life with me. I feel enriched, informed and connected.

Day 6

I am grateful that I feel a growing sense of peace, contentment, love and joy with every breath I take.

Day 7

I am grateful there is nothing to limit me except my limited thinking which I can change in the twinkling of an eye. With joyous expectation, I free my thinking, now!

March

I am grateful …A shower of truth and light surrounds me; I remember who I am!

Infinite mind creates through me now; I remember who I am!

I know what I stand for and consciously choose; I remember who I am!

My highest priorities receive my attention; I remember who I am!

Willing to express my thoughts and my feelings; I remember who I am!

Balancing desire and action, living more honestly; I remember who I am!

Doing what I love, I'm making a difference; I remember who I am!

Compassion for myself and others is my commitment; I remember who I am!

Living each moment from the inside out; I remember who I am!

My Personal Gratitude Affirmations

_____

_____

_____

_____

_____

_____

_____

_____

_____

_____

_____

_____

_____

_____

_____

_____

_____

Day 8

I am grateful that I reflect good health and vitality to my world, and feel increasingly balanced.

Day 9

I am grateful that there is a boundless source of creative ideas for me to draw from and use, and I feel wonderful in this process.

Day 10

I am grateful that everything I eat is easily digested and my body retains only that which keeps me healthy. This adds to my feeling of vibrancy!

Day 11

I am grateful that I know the value of forgiving for it is my way of healing, and returning to powerful feelings of love.

Day 12

I am grateful that I can make empowering contributions each and every day to the well-being of the planet, through my creative thoughts and actions. I feel delighted with a deepening sense of purpose.

Day 13

I am grateful that my work today is filled with unique opportunities to serve and contribute to the highest good of all. I take full advantage of those opportunities with feelings of awe and wonder.

Day 14

I am grateful that life is a blast as I conquer each mountain in my life. I am feeling stronger on my climb, every day.

March

I am grateful I access the wisdom of God and am guided and led to my most appropriate choices in the use of all my resources. I open myself to fresh approaches and new ideas for generating and accepting greatly increasing abundance. At the same time I am releasing any ideas, feelings or beliefs about limitations imposed upon me by anyone or my perceived circumstances.

God is always bringing me good, and I open my heart to recognize and embrace that good with great gratitude. In faith, knowing that all is working for my highest and best, I am staying focused on my good desires. I turn *away from* any fear or doubt, *toward* the light of illumination, balance and harmony. My faithful expectation is for my greatest good!

My Personal Gratitude Affirmations

Day 15

I am grateful that as I greet each moment with thanks, I know more fully a new and glorious day is beginning. I have a feeling of vital, joy-filled expectancy.

Day 16

I am grateful that my judgments may be hidden parts of my personality and so I am opening myself to new reflections and understandings. I am feeling more compassionate and less judgmental toward others and myself.

Day 17

I am grateful that as I continue to think creatively, and with feelings of assurance, limitless possibilities are becoming more apparent.

Day 18

I am grateful that I see my health, happiness and well-being as my secrets to success. I am feeling masterful and complete.

Day 19

I am grateful that life's challenges energize my spirit and awaken me to ever expanding adventures. As a result I feel increasingly vibrant.

Day 20

I am grateful that my inner child reminds me to laugh, to sing and to have fun. I feel more balanced as I create my happy childhood, today!

Day 21

I am grateful that I am a unique expression of God and that I live in that consciousness each day. Knowing this truth I feel inspired.

March

I am grateful God is my comforter and my guide. The Presence is my armor, my amore'. I have all the resources, knowledge, training and skills which I need to handle my current situations. I claim my intuition and clarity which leads me to exactly the right approach with each person with whom I interact. There is no *them*, there is only God expressing uniquely as each individualized person. Each is doing his or her best at the time. I remember and claim my innate power, compassionately directed. All is well.

My Personal Gratitude Affirmations

Day 22

I am grateful that I am choosing to be healthier, stronger and happier, today and each day forward.

Day 23

I am grateful that the roller coaster of life's constant changes gives me a feeling of strength, endurance, excitement and success.

Day 24

I am grateful that I am beginning to build the foundation for tomorrow's actions and results. I am filled with confidence and assurance.

Day 25

I am grateful that I am bursting through any illusion of boundaries which I may have created with false beliefs. I am feeling calm and composed.

Day 26

I am grateful that my life is full of exciting outcomes providing opportunities for me to express myself with feelings of joy.

Day 27

I am grateful that I can look in the mirror and see magnificent health and feel energized by doing so.

Day 28

I am grateful that life's challenges become my opportunities to develop my strengths and thereby I feel more empowered in life.

March

I am grateful I am feeling increasing compassion and understanding in my relationships. I know I am only responsible for my own experience. At the same time, I am holding the vision of companionships that are reciprocal and filled with love, balance, compassion and vitalizing joy.

"Understanding" means to "stand under." I affirm that I have God-Love as my foundation, standing under, over, around and within me right now. From this place of God-Love, I am able to hold fast to my vision for a compassionate relationship. From a deeply felt affirmation: "I am *being loving intelligence* in action," I am holding the space for my ultimate good to demonstrate. I am releasing all that is unlike that high vision. I am putting my attention on that which I most desire to experience and I am filled with gratitude.

My Personal Gratitude Affirmations

_____
_____
_____
_____
_____
_____
_____
_____
_____
_____
_____
_____
_____
_____
_____
_____
_____
_____
_____
_____
_____

Day 29

I am grateful that a feeling of joyous expectancy fills every fiber of my being. I anticipate only the best of outcomes.

Day 30

I am grateful I remember that this is the best time for completing my projects. As I do, I feel increasingly worthwhile and free from cluttered thoughts and feelings.

Day 31

I am grateful that there is an abundance of good in varied forms always available for my use, and this awareness makes me feel affluent.

April

I am grateful,, recognizing that there is always, ever, only one higher self, one God, and therefore I am, and everyone everywhere is *within* It *as* It, I affirm this:

I am walking…so that whoever walks beside me…
Dwells in the Presence of God…
I am listening…so that whoever speaks with me…
Knows that I hear the voice of God.
And whoever places a hand in mine is lifted.
And whoever thinks of me…is illumined with God consciousness…
I am remembering…Spirit and I are one eternally.

Thanks to Dr. Peggy Bassett for the inspiration for this affirmation.

My Personal Gratitude Affirmations

_____
_____
_____
_____
_____
_____
_____
_____
_____
_____
_____
_____
_____

Day 1

I am grateful that peace of mind is mine as I accept even more opportunities that enrich, challenge and build my faith life. In the end I feel vitalized as I calmly grow.

Day 2

I am grateful that I am making *choices* rather than *decisions* which may block alternatives. I remain flexible and there is always a way for my desires to manifest in my future. I feel fascinated by my choices.

Day 3

I am grateful that on the highway of life I am discovering the best route, and I am feeling greater clarity. I have all the road signs I need just when I need them.

Day 4

I am grateful that life's pressures encourage me to move forward to greater awareness of my assets. I am filled with understanding.

Day 5

I am grateful that joy is found as I discover relevant truths, and I am feeling increasing joy as I recognize that I *am* joy!

Day 6

I am grateful that as I am making a commitment to be more awake, aware and thoughtful today, I am also feeling relaxed, deeply calm and profoundly connected.

Day 7

I am grateful that my mind, body and spirit are healthy and I am filled with vitality and energy. In this beautiful state I am free.

April

I am grateful I remember—in the middle of all of my "stuff"—that I am a loving, powerful expression of a higher power. More importantly, I remember that greater power and divine order in the universe is always available to me.

A mourning dove reminds me of this truth. The dove never doubts that the day is here, perfect in its unfolding, and it welcomes its new experience with joy, faith and trust. The letters in the word DOVE might stand for Divine Order Vibrantly Expressing. I take the dove as a symbol, as a sign of remembrance, and with each melodious note, I tune in to the song of trust and faith being sung. I know too that *I am* a beautiful "dove," another outward sign of divine order vibrantly expressing.

My Personal Gratitude Affirmations

Day 8

I am grateful that I have a partnership with my higher self, and this partnership is flourishing with feelings of serenity. What a connection!

Day 9

I am grateful that as I gently forgive myself, I have more love and feel more empathy for others. I promise to handle my heart with care.

Day 10

I am grateful I have a commitment to stop doing that which no longer serves me, and I am beginning to practice living more affirmatively. I am filled with a feeling of freedom as I release those old chains.

Day 11

I am grateful that love is all there is. As I remember this, I am more loving and feel more compassionate.

Day 12

I am grateful that my goal for today is to move with greater flexibility and ease; mentally, emotionally and physically. I experience this goal being fulfilled and I feel more optimistic.

Day 13

I am grateful that love from the one Source of life is mirrored in the eyes of those around me, and I feel a deep sense of kinship.

Day 14

I am grateful that I increasingly accept myself for who I am, with feelings of love, strength and well-being. As challenges come, my confidence grows and the results show.

April

I am grateful I can ponder one of life's puzzles: Where is the tiny physical body that was weighed in when I was born? I was so perfect and ready to meet the world with my own gifts and talents: "Hey life! Here I am!"

As my body has grown and changed through the years, the same joy and expectancy is present, simply in a different package. This seems to be a natural progression, perfect at each step of the way, as I have been testing, learning and exploring through this adventure called life. Yet the core of my being remains the same as it was before the moment of my conception.

So it is with me now. Each day is a "birth-day"…a celebration of the unchanging thread of Spirit which wends its way through my life. Each step is perfect…as my baby form was perfect for that time, as my older-person form is perfect for this time. And the unity of my continuing re-birth threads the changes together into one whole perfect life. Again I say, "Hey life! Here I am!"

My Personal Gratitude Affirmations

_____

_____

_____

_____

_____

_____

_____

_____

_____

_____

_____

_____

_____

_____

_____

_____

_____

Day 15

I am grateful that I receive with thanksgiving and give with joy. I celebrate the divine cycle of life.

Day 16

I am grateful that I am seeing more clearly through any fog of doubt, and move forward with increasing feelings of self-confidence from my connection with God.

Day 17

I am grateful that unexpected gifts are appearing in my life and I accept them thoughtfully and with feelings of great appreciation.

Day 18

I am grateful that I take time to be quiet in this busy day and I feel renewed and refreshed as a result of my "time-out."

Day 19

I am grateful I have a real sense that this universe is my home, and that I have the ability to assist others to feel this connection. This strong sense of belonging brings comfort and peace to my soul.

Day 20

I am grateful that blessings sometimes appear in disguise, and I'm smart enough to unmask them and feel inspired by them.

Day 21

I am grateful that increasing love and wisdom is mine to use in all my relationships and I feel thankful for these gifts. They call me to my highest expression.

April

I am grateful I am a compassionate, caring and joy-filled expression of the Divine One. I align with the qualities of God's love-intelligence and I am willing to be a "love-virus" with those that I care about. By example, I am quietly mentoring my friends and family. Because I appreciate and value those with whom I am interacting, they catch the "virus" and realize their own value and worth.

As I become more open to the realization of *my* natural birthright as an expression of the higher power, I more completely radiate and share my assurance, harmony and peace. I understand that each person is on their own path of understanding. As I hold a "love-light virus" without expectation or judgment, God is guiding me. When enlightenment is shared we all move forward more confidently.

My Personal Gratitude Affirmations

_____
_____
_____
_____
_____
_____
_____
_____
_____
_____
_____
_____
_____
_____
_____
_____
_____
_____
_____
_____
_____

Day 22

I am grateful that am I discovering resources which awaken my spirit with feelings of deep wonder and adventure.

Day 23

I am grateful that I can depend on myself to get a job done. I feel trustworthy.

Day 24

I am grateful I deeply understand that joy is my natural heritage. It is who I am as I connect with the source of all joy. I am feeling that joy and expressing it right now! I am joy's fountain overflowing. Let's celebrate!

Day 25

I am grateful that I am becoming more aware of the ways that my working time is eased by my innovative creations, and I feel valuable and increasingly effective.

Day 26

I am grateful that I have everything I need to move forward in my life. What a feeling of increasing assurance!

Day 27

I am grateful that I remember "Love is where you find it!" I am feeling love and finding it everywhere I look.

Day 28

I am grateful that I see beauty in the most unexpected places today. I feel enriched in the process.

April

I am grateful One Life moves and expresses as me, as a part of its creation. I have the spiritual DNA that was present before my birth into this physical experience, and the perfection of that spiritual DNA is viable, strong, and whole.

Any true healing is in the revealing of the Spiritual Truth. I have a greater alignment with God, with my natural wholeness and perfection. God is breathing the breath of life through me. I am responding to the natural rhythm and flow of Divine energy, as I increasingly rest in confidence and ease. I have within myself, God's peace and wholeness. There is a pattern, a blueprint for re-alignment with God that is eternally available. The light of God-peace, demonstrating as my peace of mind and body is present in this moment, and all is well.

My Personal Gratitude Affirmations

_____
_____
_____
_____
_____
_____
_____
_____
_____
_____
_____
_____
_____
_____
_____
_____
_____
_____
_____
_____

Day 29

I am grateful that I am increasingly speaking with confidence and with wisdom. I am feeling more assured each day.

Day 30

I am grateful that I am finding practical ways to extend my understanding of what makes a healthy family. I am feeling nurtured, loved and valued.

May

I am grateful as I speak my word of acceptance I step into exciting experiences and beginnings. My mind and heart are open to the creativity of Spirit that is expressing in new and surprising ways. I am open to guidance as to my next choices, knowing that all is unfolding for my ultimate highest good. Because of this assurance, I am proceeding with joyful confidence and peace of mind.

My Personal Gratitude Affirmations

Day 1

I am grateful that as I end the last chapter in this story of my life, I know it is really the first chapter in an altogether new book. I feel excited about my prospects and possibilities.

Day 2

I am grateful that I can share my talents exuberantly, positively and generously with those I touch, and in giving I too receive rich rewards. I feel abundantly blessed in the whole process.

Day 3

I am grateful that outer conditions have no power in my life for I have an awesome inner guidance system. I am feeling masterful and well directed.

Day 4

I am grateful that I realize; as I think and feel, so I create. Therefore I am careful with my thoughts and my feelings, and I feel vibrant.

Day 5

I am grateful that I have no need to compare myself with others. I am unique, I make a valuable contribution to life and I feel composed.

Day 6

I am grateful that something as simple as my smile opens many doors and hearts, and I feel happy and delighted by this.

Day 7

I am grateful that I am letting my light from within shine outward and it lights my day and my way. I am never lost when I stand in Divine light and I feel constantly inspired.

May

I am grateful the very earth vibrates with the creative energy of the One life, One power, One presence. In the sound and the silence it speaks of the limitless potentiality of all existence.

I feel and know that this One is blessing, singing and dancing through and as me as Spirit-energy-love. Every change and choice I make is blessed. Conscious and creative connections are appearing in my life as miracles of transformation. I am becoming clearer about my divinity and power. An even greater abundance of resources are being shared with me. I understand that I *can* use this power for good, and I *am* doing it!

My Personal Gratitude Affirmations

_____

_____

_____

_____

_____

_____

_____

_____

_____

_____

_____

_____

_____

_____

_____

_____

_____

_____

_____

_____

_____

_____

_____

Day 8

I am grateful that my mind is an overflowing storehouse for positive, powerful and productive ideas. These stimulate my creative mind to new and exciting possibilities.

Day 9

I am grateful that as I focus my attention, all of my projects are easily handled in a timely manner prompting a feeling of accomplishment.

Day 10

I am grateful that everything I eat and drink nourishes and supports my empowered way of living. I experience feelings of being nurtured.

Day 11

I am grateful that there are many colors which stimulate, balance and harmonize my day, and I sense the beauty around me. Color makes life so rich and wonderful.

Day 12

I am grateful that I am committing to find time in each day to play. I feel enriched by the freedom from concerns and the complete abandonment of my cares.

Day 13

I am grateful that seeds of ideas spring forth into full bloom and I enjoy the bouquet. My feelings of creativity blossom into beauty.

Day 14

I am grateful that I am free to express myself as God creates through me. I enjoy a deep sense of appreciation and compassion for all with whom I come in contact. I feel a powerful sense of *Oneness*.

May

I am grateful I am moving with the flexibility, ease and harmony of the God essence that fills me. My strength and stamina flow easily through and express uniquely as me. It is God's strength and stamina individualized in me.

No tension, concern or worry about my physical body has any place in my life. Right now I am stepping lightly, realizing that my joy, love and faith in the wholeness of Spirit is my "spiritual medicine" to be taken in regular "doses." My natural wisdom regarding the use of other techniques or medicines that may assist me to remain in this ease-of-motion and relaxed state, are simply another expression of the Divine intelligence, peace and Love in action. I am being guided and directed each peaceful step of the way. As God is everywhere, God is present in every approach to a greater realization of my well-being.

My Personal Gratitude Affirmations

Day 15

I am grateful that I am assured all of my needs and desires are being taken care of by God. I feel gently supported.

Day 16

I am grateful that I can enjoy the conveniences that make my life easy and efficient. I use each with a feeling of thoughtfulness in the process.

Day 17

I am grateful that I have many varied opportunities to interact with others in affirming ways. I feel that I am a positive force in my circle of life.

Day 18

I am grateful that my body has all the physical defenses necessary to insure good health. I nurture and protect these defenses through healthful ways of living. As result I feel even stronger.

Day 19

I am grateful that I communicate powerfully and lives are affected positively. I feel humbled as others claim their own worth.

Day 20

I am grateful that I have an abundance of good which flows to me in the form of gifts and cash for my good use. I am feeling worthy of this good.

Day 21

I am grateful that many forms of the written word stimulate my ideas and affirm my choices. I feel renewed.

May

I am grateful that with great joy I attune my awareness, and celebrate knowing that God is all there is. And so I must be, and everyone everywhere must be, within, surrounded by, and embraced by that wholeness.

My higher power responds with a resounding "Yes!" as I affirm only the best for each individual, whatever the form and expressions of their life.

"Yes!" To overflowing abundance and richness of blessings for every place recognized as holy ground (for as God is everywhere, then *everywhere* is holy ground).

"Yes!" Increasing numbers of people are discovering their path of deepening understanding.

"Yes!" Love-intelligence is guiding and wisdom is at the core of each choice being made.

"Yes!" I feel the power and presence, the vibrant principle and the calm expectation of the ultimate comforter here and now.

My Personal Gratitude Affirmations

_____

_____

_____

_____

_____

_____

_____

_____

_____

_____

_____

_____

_____

_____

_____

_____

_____

_____

Day 22

I am grateful for the love generously given to me in the spirit of joy. I have a deep appreciation and I am feeling the power of compassionate synergism.

Day 23

I am grateful that there are warm, cuddly things in my life which touch and reassure the child within. I feel free and playful.

Day 24

I am grateful that I gain new insights and understandings each day which further my life. Through this, I feel more intelligent.

Day 25

I am grateful for the marvel that is my hearing that grants me the pleasures of music, poems, songs of love and all the sounds of nature. I am feeling surrounded by mysteries and beauties as I quietly listen.

Day 26

I am grateful that I am lit by the Spirit within which is the eternal flame of good and my feeling of expectation is growing.

Day 27

I am grateful that I have friends who are willing to play with me and share a healing joy. I am feeling lighter each moment.

Day 28

I am grateful that my contributions to another's life are immeasurably valuable, and I feel valued in return.

May

I am grateful as I affirm that the journey I am embarking upon is part of the process of my awakening to a greater possibility for joy in my life. Remembering that I am limitlessly creative, I understand that regardless of any appearances, each opportunity is given to me as part of my spiritual evolution.

I know that only the highest and best can result from my wise and loving choices. I also know and affirm that I have whatever skills, experience and intuition are needed for my success. Caring support and positive attention is given to me from expected and unexpected places and people. God is providing all, richly and abundantly, right now. I am proceeding with confidence and peace of mind anchored firmly in Spirit.

My Personal Gratitude Affirmations

Day 29

I am grateful that my creative talents keep expressing in fresh and original ways. I feel fascinated by the results.

Day 30

I am grateful that there are time and energy-saving methods which I am using effectively today, therefore I feel more efficient.

Day 31

I am grateful that as I joyously express thanks for each day of my life, I am feeling enriched.

June

I am grateful that in this blessed moment I allow the thoughts and feelings that arise, as I am accepting that my life is within God-life. As this is spiritual Truth, it must also be that everyone, everywhere, is within the One-God-life. My acceptance feels like bliss.

Therefore, I am expressing my joy that I am within God's joy. I realize that my joy and bliss is eternally present, ready to be claimed. I am led into paths of peace and the light of abundant, new possibilities. As bliss, joy, peace and light is true for me, it is also true about every one of God's creations.

My Personal Gratitude Affirmations

_____

_____

_____

_____

_____

_____

_____

_____

_____

_____

_____

_____

_____

_____

_____

_____

Day 1

I am grateful for all the good that comes to me and I feel the shower of God's abundance nature.

Day 2

I am grateful for the wonder of our earthly home and desire to respect and protect this beautiful environment in which I live. I have a feeling of hope, optimism and responsibility.

Day 3

I am grateful that as I give thanks for all of my senses I use them wisely with increasing joy.

Day 4

I am grateful for the opportunities that I meet each day. They give me the feeling of promise.

Day 5

I am grateful I can open my heart and let go of all past experiences that I felt had hurt me. In doing so, I am filled with healing, and I am overwhelmed with the feeling of unconditional love.

Day 6

I am grateful that no job is too big or too small. I am achieving my greatness by doing each job, one at a time, mindfully, and as a result I feel balanced.

Day 7

I am grateful that I am making the choices in each day of my life to keep my mind healthy and flexible. I am feeling encouraged.

June

I am grateful …There is a labyrinth, created with joyously gathered river rocks of many sizes, shapes, colors and textures. Along the path are random gifts of nature, twigs, dry leaves, walnuts dropped from a shading tree, sometimes stones shifted out of place by wandering wildlife. These random variations represent the conditions, issues and "opportunities for deeper spiritual development" that appear in my life, many times over, to keep me focused in spiritual practices.

In imagination, I enter the labyrinth from the east. I pause to reflect on what is to be released in my prayer-walk; any expectations, tensions, "doing-ness" for this time…perhaps judgments about certain people who have appeared as my teachers on this spiritual path.

Often the appearance is that I am close to the center, and then there is a turn, and more walk to be taken. Or it seems a far distance to the center, and suddenly I am right there!

In the middle there is a sitting stump and I rest here for a time. I am facing east, to the sunrise, to new beginnings and fresh possibilities within the limitless potentiality of Spirit. Being receptive, I prepare myself to walk out into the day's activities. I notice that I feel more connected, re-energized, more balanced, centered and filled with peace. Opening to this renewed awareness I say;

"God is all there is. God is within me, and I walk with God.

In *this* precious moment all is well!

I am grateful beyond measure.

All is released for it is complete."

My Personal Gratitude Affirmations

_____

_____

_____

_____

_____

_____

_____

_____

Day 8

I am grateful that I can laugh, cry, jump, dance, sing and make merry. I am enjoying life to its fullest!

Day 9

I am grateful that I savor the food which I eat knowing that each bite is nurturing me.

Day 10

I am grateful that as I watch the birds fly, I am lifted in freedom with a wonderful sense of soaring lightly aloft and floating on the updrafts.

Day 11

I am grateful that I am filled with love and express it joyfully to each person that I meet.

Day 12

I am grateful that I see the good in everyone and others are open to see the good in me. I am feeling respected.

Day 13

I am grateful that I am taking time to discover and "smell the flowers" of life today. I feel calmer.

Day 14

I am grateful that there are precious people in my life and I have the opportunity to tell them how much they mean to me. How honored I feel to know them.

June

I am grateful, realizing that everyone is *within God.* I rejoice in the idea that right where I am is part of the perfection and wholeness of Spirit. At the same time, I stretch outward, accepting and expressing the more abundant life. It is a "both-and" position that enables me to move ahead in confidence and enthusiastic expectation of even greater good.

There are almost always challenging appearances that may grab my attention. My gift and my declaration is that these appearances hold no power over my life, as I freely turn my compassion and my love-intelligence toward the light of greater understanding. I rest in the assurance of greatly increasing peace of mind.

God is Abundance. I am within that Abundance and so I accept my affluence in many varied forms for my ultimate good.

Spirit is Love. I am within Love, and so I rejoice in expressing my affluence of love.

The One is wisdom. I am within that wisdom and so I calmly move forward supported by the guidance, wisdom and intelligence of God.

My Personal Gratitude Affirmations

_____

_____

_____

_____

_____

_____

_____

_____

_____

_____

_____

_____

_____

_____

_____

_____

_____

Day 15

I'm grateful and I am joyous because of the many blessings which I am receiving. I feel blessed beyond measure!

Day 16

I am grateful that I am finding new ways to forgive and release judgments. I free myself as I free others and I celebrate this awareness.

Day 17

I am grateful that all of my physical functions proceed in a regular, normal cycle. I am feeling stronger each day.

Day 18

I am grateful that I am attentive to the wealth of happy surprises which the universe has for me. I am trusting in the activity of life.

Day 19

I am grateful that I have the ability to demonstrate unexpected money for my wise use, and I am feeling abundantly cared for.

Day 20

I am grateful that good, intelligent and caring people are showing up more and more as guides for me. I cherish the understanding shown.

Day 21

I am grateful that I am a vital part of planet earth. I play my role innovatively by respecting it and I feel an increasing sense of balance.

June

I am grateful that as I breathe in I center myself in my deepening understanding of the creative essence of Spirit.

Breathing in, I relax into the joy of connection, surrounded by and lifted up by Spirit.

I echo the words of affirmation shared by those who have opened themselves to a richer experience and feeling regarding the truth, "All there is, is peace within Spirit..."

Being peaceful I am acting peacefully...

Balance, harmony, wholeness and acceptance are mine...

I don't take "stuff and things" personally...

I am centering myself in harmony...

I love myself more than before...

My healing is an increasing awareness of my wholeness...

Everything that I need is provided...

In *this moment* there is peace!

I feel abundantly filled with gratitude.

My Personal Gratitude Affirmations

_____
_____
_____
_____
_____
_____
_____
_____
_____
_____
_____
_____
_____
_____
_____
_____
_____
_____
_____

Day 22

I am grateful that my heart regularly works for me and I feel its rhythm as it balances my life.

Day 23

I am grateful that the sunshine of caring people warms and soothes my mind. I am feeling more secure.

Day 24

I am grateful that today I am communicating with someone to release and heal an old hurt. I feel the cycle of kindness being experienced by both of us.

Day 25

I am grateful that as I commit to a quiet time, prayer or meditation, I am feeling renewed.

Day 26

I am grateful that there is beauty in my surroundings, and I am opening my eyes to see it all newly. I feel serene.

Day 27

I am grateful that I am able to reach out today to stay in touch with someone from my past and we share feelings of support.

Day 28

I am grateful that I can find someone to confide in today who is impartial and I feel their kindness.

June

I am grateful ...
   "Cheers!" For the many gifts and talents that are shared.
   "Hooray!" For knowing and celebrating that my joys are multiplied as I share them with others.
   "Ohm!" As I recognize more expressions of harmony, balance and peace.
   "Ah!" As I breathe in the fresh possibilities of my creativity and self expression.
   "Ah-ha!" As I deepen my understanding of the power of my thinking, my words, my feelings and my choices. I understand that these choices result in my new appreciation of *everything* I am experiencing, and my life is enriched. May I guide the tendency of my thoughts and feelings knowing *I* am creating my experiences around the appearances in my life.

My Personal Gratitude Affirmations

_____
_____
_____
_____
_____
_____
_____
_____
_____
_____
_____
_____
_____
_____
_____
_____
_____
_____

Day 29

I am grateful that I am finding clarity as I look at what it means to be friendly and express friendship. I feel more youthful in the process.

Day 30

I am grateful that I am moving forward to handle the affairs of my life with greater wisdom and deeper feelings of love.

July

I am grateful and I feel free, awed and comforted in knowing that I am, and each of God's creations are filled with, surrounded by, and live within the One.

I affirm that all have open arms, open hearts and minds, accepting the bountiful gifts which continue to be given, every moment of every day. Everything is mine to use freely, with compassionate wisdom as my natural birthright.

In great gratitude, I feel blessed! Blessed! Blessed! The seeds of my affirmations and acceptance are planted, the fruit is ripening.

My Personal Gratitude Affirmations

_____

_____

_____

_____

_____

_____

_____

_____

_____

_____

_____

_____

_____

_____

_____

Day 1

I am grateful that even in the storms of life I recognize my blessings and can feel composed and free.

Day 2

I am grateful that I am poised, confident and certain for I am established in unlimited good, and I am feeling more assured.

Day 3

I am grateful that abundance and limitless potential surrounds me and is working through me at all times. I feel satisfied with my choices.

Day 4

I am grateful that everyone I meet today is filled with increasingly radiant health, and I feel amazed at all my limitless possibilities.

Day 5

I am grateful that I am impervious to all strain and stress. I feel in greater harmony with all life.

Day 6

I am grateful that I am accepting my increasing prosperity and I am using it with wisdom.

Day 7

I am grateful that I can walk and talk with poise, and dignity and feel the peace wherever I go.

July

I am grateful that whatever my new *problitunity*, wherever my need seems to be, however I may be feeling, I am willing to affirm "I am one with God now!" I am opening to fresh perspectives, exploring my responses and my thinking.

As I am changing my consciousness, the very basic building blocks in my cells shift! Understanding this is my first step in optimum change for my life. I remember that I am a spiritual being, living in a physical universe. I am greatly blessed to know I can use my increasing spiritual awareness to spark new affirmative beginnings. New creation in my life is at hand, here and now! I relax in deep gratitude for knowing this Truth.

My Personal Gratitude Affirmations

_____
_____
_____
_____
_____
_____
_____
_____
_____
_____
_____
_____
_____
_____
_____
_____
_____
_____
_____
_____
_____
_____
_____

Day 8

I am grateful that I am lovingly sharing my resources with others. I feel contented in this divine circulation.

Day 9

I am grateful that I am in control of my experience of the world, knowing that only the highest good is my destiny. I feel God's protection as I live within the embrace of Love.

Day 10

I am grateful that as I affirm abundance, and expect abundance of prosperity as a natural part of my life, I *feel* abundant!

Day 11

I am grateful that I am working in harmony each day with everyone I meet and I feel the energy of kindness flowing bountifully.

Day 12

I am grateful that my work is increasingly easy, and I respond to every action with feelings of joy and understanding.

Day 13

I am grateful that I am creating my personal world and I am surrounded with beauty, peace and love.

Day 14

I am grateful for my life and the unique and vital activities that I enjoy each day. I feel more calm and responsive.

July

I am grateful that beyond any feelings of stress, I affirm and state with confidence, that right now, the song of summer is orchestrated to enhance my sense of connection with life. Beyond the bustle, chatter and noise of the world's perceptions and news, the beauty of creation in all its glory *must* impact my senses. I experience greatly increasing poise and confidence in the ultimate power of God for good. Even the tickle in my nose reminds me of the essence of all life and I celebrate blossoming growth all around me.

As this is true in my physical nature, it is also true in my spiritual nature. And so I affirm that there is no stress that can ultimately impinge on me. *Now,* I live, breathe, and am balanced within, and energized by God-wholeness. From this space of re-awareness, I know that achievement in my creative projects proceeds with ease, poise, love-intelligence and beauty. It is my gift in this moment, and each of the 86,400 new moments in this 24 hour day.

My Personal Gratitude Affirmations

_____
_____
_____
_____
_____
_____
_____
_____
_____
_____
_____
_____
_____
_____
_____
_____
_____
_____

Day 15

I am grateful that I am making choices based on Divine inspiration and I feel the power of that guidance.

Day 16

I am grateful that each new day brings to me eternal goodness and I celebrate with a song-filled heart.

Day 17

I am grateful that I am recognizing the perfect, complete and ever present strength within me, and I am moving forward with greater feelings of confidence.

Day 18

I am grateful that I am accepting all of the inner Power that is guiding my choices. I am feeling energized!

Day 19

I am grateful that I am thinking affirmatively, and in faith I am accepting my abundance in all good forms.

Day 20

I am grateful that there in an infinite rhythm at the center of everything and I am feeling my part in the perfect wholeness of God.

Day 21

I am grateful that my physical body is my spiritual temple and I am treating myself with dignity and loving care.

July

I am grateful as I speak my word in celebration of the limitless freedom and beauty, the joy and blessed unity experienced by each person, everywhere. Whatever the road being walked, whatever the circumstances, my gift is to remember that I am always *in* the One, and there is eternally that truth of my being wrapped in the wholeness of God. I am free to think, to feel, to make my choices and take action in confidence of the highest good. All is unfolding in its divine perfection, in the most appropriate time…God's time.

I accept the reassurance of this spiritual Truth, and shift into awareness of the freedom and creative potential that I am noticing as results in my life.

My Personal Gratitude Affirmations

_____
_____
_____
_____
_____
_____
_____
_____
_____
_____
_____
_____
_____
_____
_____
_____
_____
_____
_____
_____
_____

Day 22

I am grateful that my world is opening to new horizons and I am eagerly moving forward to even greater successes.

Day 23

I am grateful that I am enjoying life with a healthy mind and body. I am feeling more balanced each day.

Day 24

I am grateful for understanding that whatever I see and believe becomes my experience and my reality. I am awed by this principle of life.

Day 25

I am grateful that I am reaping the benefits of an affirmative outlook in life. I feel empowered.

Day 26

I am grateful that whatever I do, wherever I go, I am expecting the highest and best in my experience.

Day 27

I am grateful that I delight in helping others and I am rewarded by the richness of the outcome.

Day 28

I am grateful that any task, large or small, is worth doing to the best of my ability at the time, and I am a winner.

July

I am grateful I understand that I am mostly made up of water. This makes it easy for me to think and feel, that the same wholeness represented by the deep and broad river of God-Love, is within, surrounding, embracing, and cradling every person everywhere.

Whatever my opportunities, God-love is my guiding wisdom. Wherever there is unease, God-love is the soothing balm to my soul. Whatever the challenge, God-love is my powerful creative Source. Whatever the celebration, God-love is the Divine energy and Presence. Wherever there is the feeling of lack or limitation of any form, God-love is the abundant Power and intelligence directing me. Whatever my question, God-love is the answer.

With an overwhelming sense of expectation of the highest good unfolding here and now, I say, "Thank you God!"

My Personal Gratitude Affirmations

_____
_____
_____
_____
_____
_____
_____
_____
_____
_____
_____
_____
_____
_____
_____
_____
_____
_____
_____
_____

Day 29

I am grateful that I have a strong and healthy body and I'm feeling increasingly more vibrant and youthful today.

Day 30

I am grateful that I am basking in the love of life, and I'm feeling more loving and balanced.

Day 30

I am grateful that there are physical lights to brighten my path, and spiritual lights to light my life. In this awareness I feel at-one within the presence of God.

August

I am grateful as I relish the myriad sounds of nature I feel the kiss and energy of sunlight and breeze. I taste and smell the very essence of life. My eyes feast on the glories that God has wrought. I soar as the eagle and dance a ballet as the dragonfly. I am there in an instant, and "it's perfect!"

My Personal Gratitude Affirmations

Day 1

I am grateful that I am letting the miracles of love and life take place in my life and I am filled with wonder.

Day 2

I am grateful that I am gently releasing any desire for food or drink that is not beneficial to my body. I feel masterful!

Day 3

I am grateful that I am finding ways to acknowledge myself and my friends today. I feel empowered.

Day 4

I am grateful that there is enough love in me that goes out to others, in confidence that the cycle of love returns to me and I feel enriched.

Day 5

I am grateful that I am committing my life to harmonious living in all my daily activities. I am feeling stronger in the process.

Day 6

I am grateful that I am making my own "luck" by taking advantage of every opportunity to grow. I feel enriched by this wisdom.

Day 7

I am grateful that my life is increasingly healthy and I am filled with greater energy.

August

I am grateful I recognize I am dancing in the light and shadows and my eyes are composing one-of-a-kind mental images. I am traveling the world through these pictures…they express joy, childlike playfulness, serenity, harmony, a unique perspective on life. I am opening windows on potential dreams. "It's perfect!"

My Personal Gratitude Affirmations

_____

_____

_____

_____

_____

_____

_____

_____

_____

_____

_____

_____

_____

_____

_____

_____

_____

_____

_____

_____

_____

_____

_____

_____

_____

_____

_____

_____

_____

Day 8

I am grateful that when I speak I am heard. When I listen, I hear with my heart and feel compassion.

Day 9

I am grateful that I don't have to struggle or wrestle with life. I am finding positive ways to rise to the top of my experiences. I feel I am overcoming old beliefs.

Day 10

I am grateful that I have an abundance of gifts to share. In the sharing I am made richer…it's a natural result, and I feel renewed.

Day 11

I am grateful that I am beginning to understand that any fear I may have is simply my faith misdirected. In confident expectation, I am focusing my attention on the results I want in my life.

Day 12

I am grateful that I am finding innovative ways to say "thank you" today and I feel appreciated in return.

Day 13

I am grateful that there are surprising numbers of people to assist me when I ask. I am feeling the synergy and support of God working through others.

Day 14

I am grateful that music touches, soothes and heals me with its deep rhythms and I feel the vitalizing vibrations.

August

I am grateful I am moving forward with my highest intention, following my bliss, guided by my unique, individualized intelligence and love. I am expressing joy that I am *in* God's joy. As I realize that my bliss is eternally present, ready to be claimed, I am led into paths of peace and the light of abundant, new possibilities. This is true for me and it is true for every one of God's creations. Intelligence guided by compassion, empathy and love works miracles. I have an over-whelming sense of gratitude for this truth, and the opportunity to speak it. "It's perfect!"

My Personal Gratitude Affirmations

Day 15

I am grateful that I am letting the miracle of love and life take place here and now, with great feelings of connection and meaning.

Day 16

I am grateful that I am opening myself to accept more gifts that others wish to share with me. I set aside any judgment about the gifts and receive them with joy.

Day 17

I am grateful that I am breathing easily and I am accomplishing much with feelings of trust.

Day 18

I am grateful that I love to express my gratitude to those around me, and we are all enriched. In the exchange I feel more expansive and light.

Day 19

I am grateful that I am willing to explore any resistance to change and move ahead with greater faith and wisdom. My feelings of success are growing.

Day 20

I am grateful that I can appreciate the beauty in the creations of man and nature, and I feel refreshed.

Day 21

I am grateful that I am safe in the knowledge that my inner self is providing me with a great guidance system and I feel secure.

August

I am grateful that simply by being me, day by day, I am choosing to live life more fully and abundantly, in tune with limitless possibilities. I am opening my doors of understanding. Through my innocent, yet wise and enthusiastic example, I am inviting others to move through life to their own spiritual discoveries. It's perfect!

My Personal Gratitude Affirmations

Day 22

I am grateful that there are attractive and caring people in my daily life. I can easily express my feelings of appreciation to them.

Day 23

I am grateful that information and entertainment from many varied sources enlightens me and I feel inspired.

Day 24

I am grateful that I am warmed and comforted through my contacts with others. I feel cheered by these thoughts.

Day 25

I am grateful that everyday choices are leading me successfully to new possibilities and solutions. I am feeling very creative today.

Day 26

I am grateful that I am always being guided to the right professionals who are willing and able to assist me. I increasingly trust this process.

Day 27

I am grateful that intelligence and love are the foundations of my being, and I am using these qualities well. I feel excited about delightful new opportunities for my growth.

Day 28

I am grateful that many things are reminding me every day, of the blessings and gifts in my life. I feel amused by some of the "messengers" that get my attention.

August

I am grateful that through my many "opportunities for growth," my joy and my pain, and my commitment to use every particle of sensory information I was given, I trust my inner Guidance. Faith is leading me to find a way to spiritual truth, to light, to Love, to peace. As difficult as my path may have seemed in the past, there have been no mistakes. When I close my eyes for the last time, I will know beyond any doubt, "It's all been perfect!"

My Personal Gratitude Affirmations

_____

_____

_____

_____

_____

_____

_____

_____

_____

_____

_____

_____

_____

_____

_____

_____

_____

_____

_____

_____

_____

_____

_____

_____

_____

_____

Day 29

I am grateful that as the weather changes, I too change in my expansion and growth. I feel fascinated by the unfolding scene.

Day 30

I am grateful that there is one God-energy which is the source of my energy, and I rejoice in my use of it.

Day 31

I am grateful that as rainbows symbolize the eternal promise of good, I see rainbows in the lives of people around me. I can feel the vibrations of peace and promise.

September

I am grateful I am one with the harmony and patterns of perfection in God's world. Expansive peace is my key to success today. I have an overflowing sense of interconnection with each person I meet. Enthusiasm unlocks my personal door to loving relationships. There is only Divine-peace and it manifests in each cell of my body.

My Personal Gratitude Affirmations

Day 1

I am grateful that I know high performance is an "inside job," which then appears in my daily life and I feel the power.

Day 2

I am grateful that I am motivated to organize my ideas and living space today. I am feeling more clarity and balance.

Day 3

I am grateful that as I read, I have new understandings and discover unique pathways for action. My creativity is surprising!

Day 4

I am grateful that I am finding time today to relax, meditate, and touch a deeper calm than ever before. I feel more serene, as if I'm resting in a quiet mountain-top meadow.

Day 5

I am grateful that I willingly notice any unease and use it as a wake-up call for creative action. As a result I feel more powerful and in control!

Day 6

I am grateful that support is walking through the door right now by way of some surprising channels and I feel more trusting. What I need is usually arriving right on time.

Day 7

I am grateful that I am more willing to use pain as a signal to adjust something in my mind or body, and I feel more hopeful.

September

I am grateful that life's challenges become my opportunities for peaceful living. Serendipity (dipping into life with serenity) is my key to success. I look in the mirror and see health and balance reflected back to me. I am *enactive* and *responsive,* rather than *reactive.* I allow my inner and outer selves to communicate creatively. I am willing to take an adventurous approach to life with an expectation of greater good. I express myself with joy, enthusiasm and vitality.

My Personal Gratitude Affirmations

Day 8

I am grateful that when I make choices, it is an affirmation of the possibility for my greater good, and I feel worthy!

Day 9

I am grateful that prosperity is showing up in varied and unexpected packages. I am accepting that delivery with satisfaction!

Day 10

I am grateful that I am handling repayment of my "financial agreements" (my debts) more easily and in a timely manner. I am feeling more secure.

Day 11

I am grateful that my immune system is healthy and active. I am celebrating my good health!

Day 12

I am grateful that I am blessing my past, the people in it, and all the lessons they have taught me. Harmony is my feeling, now!

Day 13

I am grateful that today I am letting my inner kid out to playfully re-create. I have such a feeling of joy!

Day 14

I am grateful that I am willing to laugh and release any tensions that may have built up in my muscles. I feel more relaxed, flexible and strong!

September

I am grateful I know *God is* "the infinite companion," always love, always responding, "Yes, my beloved!" God is the ultimate Creator, and the harvest is the great creation.

How awesome and comforting to rest in knowing I am, and each of God's beings is filled with, surrounded by, and lives within the One.

I affirm that all people have open arms, open hearts and minds, accepting the bountiful gifts which continue to be given, every moment of every day. Everything is mine to use with compassionate wisdom as my natural birthright.

In great gratitude, I remember I am blessed! Blessed! Blessed! The seeds of affirmation and acceptance are planted, the fruit is ripening. The harvest is ready!

My Personal Gratitude Affirmations

Day 15

I am grateful that money is flowing abundantly to my household for all good uses. I am feeling more confident!

Day 16

I am grateful that I am resolving any conflicts in my interactions and relationships, with compassion and understanding. I am embracing my inner peace!

Day 17

I am grateful that any "cuts" in my emotional or physical life are healing beautifully. I feel healthier and more vitally alive today!

Day 18

I am grateful that I am enjoying gracious living and I give thanks for each day of my life. I am feeling more content.

Day 19

I am grateful that I see conflict as "a diamond in the rough" that needs to be polished with love and understanding. This is a fascinating prospect.

Day 20

I am grateful that I willingly involve those around me in the successes I am enjoying, and this feels delightful!

Day 21

I am grateful that I am savoring each moment of my life for the love and energy that emanates in, through and around me. I feel more loving each day to every person that I meet.

September

I am grateful I am acknowledging the limitless potential for peace which now exists and I accept my daily portion. In this moment I touch the peace center of my being through the life-thread of my breathing. Openly and with joy I embrace all overtures for peaceful communications.

My Personal Gratitude Affirmations

_____
_____
_____
_____
_____
_____
_____
_____
_____
_____
_____
_____
_____
_____
_____
_____
_____
_____
_____
_____
_____
_____
_____
_____
_____
_____
_____

Day 22

I am grateful that the joy and pleasure of a healthy mind and body are my birthright. I feel excited!

Day 23

I am grateful that the more I give, the more I receive. I really enjoy giving from my feeling of "more than enough!"

Day 24

I am grateful that the pleasures of love, life and abundance surround me and are incorporated into my life each day. I am feeling more energetic!

Day 25

I am grateful that my new ideas are like bubbles of champagne bursting forth with the celebration of energy and life.

Day 26

I am grateful that I am savoring each moment of my life rather than racing to see how quickly I can get to the end of it. I feel the benefits of this wisdom.

Day 27

I am grateful that as I encounter any barriers which appear like a wall of darkness, I step past them into the light of new possibilities. I feel more in control today.

Day 28

I am grateful that as I am resolutely looking upon my "non-friends" with compassion, understanding love overcomes all adversity, they may become my "friends." I feel serene in my intention.

September

I am grateful that in every situation there is love, peace and harmony. My good in life takes nothing away from anyone. God's good expresses for me as joyous fulfillment now. In every conversation I exemplify God's love in action. God's intelligence acts through me in wise and loving ways. Today is another experience in the unfolding of my God-expression. I am acting and speaking with compassion, therefore, I am always appropriate. "I am kindness in action" is my mantra for today.

My Personal Gratitude Affirmations

Day 29

I am grateful I understand that beauty is in the eyes of the beholder. I am seeing beauty in those around me and I feel more awake and aware.

Day 30

I am grateful that my opportunities are becoming clearer as I remember that my higher self is the Source of my good. I am claiming the Divine wisdom and guidance of God!

October

I am grateful ... My heart beats with the One-God heart—
I meet others in the circle of life.
Light and space, colors and shapes seem to define,
Yet abundant energy creates a swirl of unity and love.
This is the Truth beyond time.

My Personal Gratitude Affirmations

Day 1

I am grateful that I have money to use wisely, to share and to spare. It is my opportunity to demonstrate generosity and grace.

Day 2

I am grateful that the answers to my questions are providing new perspectives and limitless possibilities, so I feel more creative.

Day 3

I am grateful that I am finding exactly the right words to express my thoughts and feelings, now. I feel stimulated and confident!

Day 4

I am grateful that I have many resources to support my ideas and creations. I recognize the value of these unusual gifts.

Day 5

I am grateful that there is plenty of time for me to accomplish all that needs to be done and I feel playful!

Day 6

I am grateful that there are systems which I use every day to keep myself organized and feeling sane. As a result, I am feeling more balanced.

Day 7

I am grateful that many people are mirrors in my life to reflect back to me clear thoughts. This is a fascinating process that makes life run more smoothly.

October

I am grateful I am reminded to notice where I am making my spiritual investments. As the material world changes constantly and "fear-casts" try to ensnare my mind and feelings, it is most important that I turn my attention with faith toward the ultimate Truth of an abundant Source. Coming from a commitment to express compassion and love, I am filled with the resources to be a true friend. I am available to assist when it is beneficial, and to share the spiritual Truth in challenging situations. From this place I am, and everyone is, able to live a more successful life in the richest sense of the word.

With this light on my "alter of faith," I speak my word and feel bathed in this enlightenment: FAITH: Focusing Attention in the Holy (Holy=Wholeness) is the key that unlocks my successful living "portfolio." This spiritual investment pays great dividends!

For this Truth of knowing and the opportunity to re-center in this FAITH investment, I am grateful.

My Personal Gratitude Affirmations

_____

_____

_____

_____

_____

_____

_____

_____

_____

_____

_____

_____

_____

_____

_____

_____

_____

_____

Day 8

I am grateful that my productivity is endless and I gladly share the results with others. I am feeling thankful and proud!

Day 9

I am grateful that my intimate relationship with myself aids my relationship with others. This synergy supports everyone.

Day 10

I am grateful that my body functions regularly and effectively to maintain my active life style. In this moment I feel lighter.

Day 11

I am grateful that I have a mental book of photographs that remind me of my successes and support my movement forward. I feel so thankful!

Day 12

I am grateful that I am using my full power and am guided by my inner wisdom. I feel energized and enthusiastic!

Day 13

I am grateful that I am resting in quiet confidence, balance and poise and I feel more awake and aware.

Day 14

I am grateful that I am safely and easily moving from one life destination to another. I know I'm appreciated on this journey.

October

I am grateful life is full of ripples of possibility. I think of a still lake that has a single droplet of rain that dots its surface. That is the beginning of a ripple. That is what my ideas do. They drop into the stillness of my mind and begin to ripple out into new experiences, new possibilities for increasing compassion and greatness in my life.

If it is rather than there being just a single drop, I can imagine all the ripples as my love going out into the world. What a gift for every one of us!

My Personal Gratitude Affirmations

_____
_____
_____
_____
_____
_____
_____
_____
_____
_____
_____
_____
_____
_____
_____
_____
_____
_____
_____
_____
_____
_____
_____
_____
_____
_____

Day 15

I am grateful that there is a loving presence that is supplying me with all of my good, and I feel that my possibilities are endless.

Day 16

I am grateful that I am releasing every tension in my mind and body and am walking more freely each day.

Day 17

I am grateful that the peace and power of a divine presence is always within me. This sense increases my peaceful feelings.

Day 18

I am grateful that I enthusiastically accept the possibility of creating increasing harmony in my life. I am feeling more balanced.

Day 19

I am grateful that I am meeting each new situation with feelings of confidence and assurance.

Day 20

I am grateful that I am poised and feeling more prosperous, accepting the gifts that have already been given by God.

Day 21

I am grateful that as I relax, I remember that God-peace is my peace within.

October

I am grateful the Divine Source of all creation is all there is.

Just as athletes focus their high intention, take appropriate actions, and then *release* the outcome as they prepare for their next steps, so I affirm and know that I am using this same strategy as my spiritual practice.

In reviewing the past, winners focus on their successes, on that which moves them ahead. I am also putting my attention and loving energy on my past experiences and the events which are the most productive to all my relationship activities. In my family, this love-practice results only in "winners" with no "losers!" What a blessing!

My Personal Gratitude Affirmations

Day 22

I am grateful that I am living within the vitality of God. Every cell in my body vibrates with joy, energy and ease.

Day 23

I am grateful that I am expressing the creativity of Spirit, and I feel joyous in my demonstrations.

Day 24

I am grateful that I am opening myself to receive more abundance in varied ways, from God's limitless storehouse. I am singing like a bird from a feeling of joyous over-flow.

Day 25

I am grateful that I have an inner compass that is guiding me to a deeper awareness of beauty and awe of nature. I am feeling greatly blessed.

Day 26

I am grateful that I am having the opportunity to meet new people who are enriching my life and bring me discoveries and laughter.

Day 27

I am grateful that I as I attune to the waves on the river of life, I feel washed by the feeling of strength and refreshment and rocked in the arms of God.

Day 28

I am grateful that every new commitment that I make is bringing me to a greater realization of the unusual ways that God-Love is supporting me. I am feeling more secure each moment.

October

I am grateful today is a fresh new beginning. It's very possible that I may be only part of the way through my physical lifetime. I imagine all that I may encounter as I stretch and expand the expression of the divine, uniquely individualized spirit that I am. This is an awesome speculation on all I may yet do. I am only limited by my beliefs "up until now," so I consciously affirm, "I am free to be all that I can be!"

My Personal Gratitude Affirmations

Day 29

I am grateful that the peace and Divine order of God is in charge of all my activities, so I feel increasingly powerful.

Day 30

I am grateful that I feel at peace with a touch, a smile, a gesture or a word of caring. I feel the compassion coming to me.

Day 31

I am grateful that the vitality of God flows through my body and my affairs, so I feel stronger, freer and more whole.

November

I am grateful God is all there is; the One power, Divine presence, the Creator, the Love-intelligence that flows through and as me, in this precious moment. I celebrate my opportunities to deepen and expand my awareness that I am living within God-life, and God-life is within me. My life is enriched and for this truth, I am so thankful. I know that the gifts of God have already been bestowed, and that my life is lighter and more grace-filled.

My Personal Gratitude Affirmations

Day 1

I am grateful that I am being lovingly guided through each of the choices that I am making, so I feel protected.

Day 2

I am grateful that as I release any ill thoughts I may have had against anyone who I thought had hurt, annoyed or confused me, I feel freer! I refuse to misunderstand or be misunderstood and that feels great!

Day 3

I am grateful that there is one master peacemaker, God-within me. Peace is flowing through me, and I feel it, now!

Day 4

I am grateful that there is infinite prosperity available to me and I open myself to claim it enthusiastically!

Day 5

I am grateful that I am joyously embracing my life that is filled with vitality, energy and greater feelings of power.

Day 6

I am grateful that I am releasing any sense of depression or fear, and I am entering my world today with confidence.

Day 7

I am grateful that I am reaping the rewards of prosperity as I am seeing through the illusion of lack. I am rich beyond measure!

November

I am grateful...
"Praise God from whom all blessings flow..."
I count my blessings as I go
From day to day, and live my life
My eyes on joy instead of strife.

My blessings multiply and then
One gift is two, and later ten—
As I acknowledge God as Source
My life becomes a richer course—

A flood of kindness rushing by,
A life-force there for me to try.
My "random acts" return to bless,
And beauty all around does press.

I open up my floodgates now—
A loving God does show me how.
I accept the richness there for me,
God's Love is Life, and that I see!

My Personal Gratitude Affirmations

_____
_____
_____
_____
_____
_____
_____
_____
_____
_____
_____
_____

Day 8

I am grateful that today I am feeling joy and thanksgiving for all the love and prosperity in my life.

Day 9

I am grateful that I am placing no limits on my goals, my objectives or my ideas. I feel daring and assured of success!

Day 10

I am grateful that everything blesses me and I am blessing everything. This is my secret to feeling balanced and empowered.

Day 11

I am grateful that my relationships with those I most love are open, honest, and expressive of respect, compassion and feelings of care.

Day 12

I am grateful that I am a healthy, vibrant, enthusiastic and loving person.

Day 13

I am grateful that my life is limitless and filled with grand ideas ready to be actualized. I am feeling excited.

Day 14

I am grateful that I enjoy each day of my life and have a zest for living.

November

I am grateful I realize the spiritual Truth, that God is all there is. God is my Soul-Partner and I know that whatever the challenge that has been appearing up-until-now has no energy to remain. I have learned whatever there is to learn from this creative opportunity. Whatever I am to do for any completion is becoming known, and I am able and willing to take those steps for release. There is no tomorrow about this issue, there is only a release *now!* As I pay attention to the greater good that I desire, that which has held my attention with anxiety, concern, or perhaps fear, disappears as simply as the fog lifts with the warmth of the sun's rays. My affirmation of *now* is gently allowing me to have a greater vision and ease of living. In great gratitude I remember that each breath is a breath of new life, God's life. Each beat of my heart is a reminder of the ever-present love-energy that reveals the spiritual Truth of my being. The *challenge* has no more power, and is released into its nothingness.

For this truth, I am so thankful. I know that the gifts of God have already been given, and that my life is lighter and more joyous.

My Personal Gratitude Affirmations

Day 15

I am grateful that I am making heaven happen here and now through my right thinking and my feelings of joy.

Day 16

I am grateful that I see praise-worthy qualities in those with whom I work, and acknowledge their work well done. I feel thoughtful and at ease.

Day 17

I am grateful that I am opening my mind to the thoughts of others, for they too have a right to their beliefs and perspectives. I feel a deep respect and openness for all.

Day 18

I am grateful I understand that my body is the place where I live, so I carefully choose my food, my drink, my exercise and my experiences. I feel energized!

Day 19

I am grateful that each person walks on parallel paths with others, and I feel love and respect for all on our unique spiritual journeys.

Day 20

I am grateful that there is increasing peace and good will everywhere and I feel a part of it.

Day 21

I am grateful that I am remaining conscious of the environment and am doing my share in keeping it clean, healthy and balanced. I feel the importance of this awareness.

November

I am grateful ...

If "Thank You" is my only prayer, said many times a day,
Thoughtfulness then spreads around, compassion is my way.

If "Thank You" is my only prayer, perhaps it is enough
To help a friend whose path in life is temporarily rough.

If "Thank You" is my only prayer, and spoken with a smile,
Perhaps it's just what is needed...for someone's extra mile.

If "Thank You" is my only prayer, thankful within the One,
Then I stay in loving kindness...no battles to be won.

If "Thank You" is my only prayer, and gratefulness my game,
Cycles of love throughout the world...harmony is my aim!

If "Thank You" is my only prayer...
"Thank You! Thank You! Thank You!"
Quietly, I rest in joy. There's nothing else to do!

My Personal Gratitude Affirmations

Day 22

I am grateful that I know nothing can disturb me unless I let it. I am choosing to open my mind and heart only to feelings of harmony.

Day 23

I am grateful that I am sending love messages and feelings to everyone I meet and think of throughout my day.

Day 24

I am grateful that I am staying awake to the fragility and beauty of our environment, and I am doing what I can to honor it. I am feeling more assured about the outcomes.

Day 25

I am grateful that I am greeting this day with a cleansed mind and I am feeling more free-spirited.

Day 26

I am grateful that I am opening my heart to all that empowers me as I go through my day feeling the richness of my blessings.

Day 27

I am grateful that the life energy of my body and mind are in harmony and balance, and I feel this with trust and enthusiasm!

Day 28

I am grateful that I am enjoying the feeling of freedom of choice in all that I think, say and do.

November

I am grateful I know that the master teacher, Jesus of Nazareth, taught that by following his example I would have life more abundantly. Biblical writings also remind me that there is a spiritual principle that it *is* done unto me *as* I believe. Through the ages, other religious teachers have also spoken of this power of belief. Therefore, knowing that I live in God's abundant universe, I set aside any world views of limitation and step confidently into God's limitless storehouse of good. In gratitude, I joyously accept my blessings in many varied forms, right here and right now. Life is good and very good!

My Personal Gratitude Affirmations

Day 29

I am grateful that I know; to love is to feel love. To be loved is to soar unto the heavens. I am feeling both loving and loved.

Day 30

I am grateful that as I remember joy is a creation from inside me, I feel an overwhelming sense of expansiveness and expectancy.

December

I am grateful... "Peace, be still and know that I am God." A wise teacher many years ago startled me when she said, "You can't get any more peace than you have right now!" She then went on to remind me that all the peace there can be is right inside me. God is peace, and God is always within, surrounding and moving through me, as me. So in times of challenge and joy, my affirmation is, "God's peace is my peace... God's peace is my peace...God's peace is my peace...God's peace is my peace!"

My Personal Gratitude Affirmations

Day 1

I am grateful that I am focusing my thoughts and expectations on *much, more, good* and *better*. My life shows the results and I enjoy deep feelings of appreciation.

Day 2

I am grateful that my body possesses infinite vitality. I am strong and I feel resilient and full of energy.

Day 3

I am grateful that I am living this day fearlessly and successfully and I feel greater love flowing to me like a lovely river.

Day 4

I am grateful that I cheer at other's successes, knowing and feeling that my successes are thrilling too.

Day 5

I am grateful that I have many opportunities to share love with others, and I am reaching out more each day to share my feelings of compassion.

Day 6

I am grateful that I increasingly accept the idea that *everything* is a gift and a blessing, even when I don't recognize it at first. I feel calmer from this perspective.

Day 7

I am grateful that I am surrounded by creative people who stimulate the best ideas in me and I experience a deep sense of satisfaction.

December

I am filled with assurance, knowing everyone everywhere is sourced by a Divine loving God, the Creative Spirit.

I open myself to a deeper awareness of the limitless potential for expression of this inner light and love. Beyond any data or appearance, there is the Creative Presence doing its work of peace and joy. I celebrate the inner illumination that is shining forth into the world through so many unique expressions of Spirit. This light blesses all that it touches. I rest balanced and at peace, knowing this truth.

My Personal Gratitude Affirmations

Day 8

I am grateful that as I am a friend, I am attracting true friends and I feel more satisfied.

Day 9

I am grateful for understanding that healing comes in many forms. Sometimes something must be released before natural wholeness can be revealed, and so I "let go" and live.

Day 10

I am grateful that there is an unchanging creative power and presence in the world for good. I can access it with my empowering thoughts and feelings!

Day 11

I am grateful that there are seasons of my life, and each season is bringing new awareness and feelings of great blessings.

Day 12

I am grateful that as I reach out and communicate with someone from my past, I am feeling enriched by that connection.

Day 13

I am grateful that I have experienced many ways that can be used to accomplish a project. Used with a feeling of success, each approach has its advantages. As I let go of the need to be "right" I feel more creative.

Day 14

I am grateful that I know "God's will" is for my good. Ultimately, I am recognizing my highest good and I am feeling a sense of joy and trust.

December

I am grateful I know that forgiveness is the gift I give myself. It is only when I continue to look into the past expecting to have a different outcome, that I have feelings of regret, sorrow, anger or even revenge.

I am learning that forgiveness is the act of freeing *myself* not another. Forgiveness does not condone anything that was done or said, nor does it mean that someone else "wins" and I "lose." It does not mean that I was *bad*. Every time that I return to the old story, I am disempowering myself. In essence we have been taught, "Judge not or you will be judged". And so with an expectation of increasing peace of mind, I am releasing my old judgments.

As I celebrate my life today with compassion, I am empowered and I am truly a winner. Now I am more able to move ahead with my life in joy. I am giving *myself* the gift of forgiveness every day, and I *am* the gift of love expressing.

My Personal Gratitude Affirmations

Day 15

I am grateful that my breath and my heartbeat always remind me of my connection with God. I feel I am living my "heaven within."

Day 16

I am grateful that I remember; the only real time is *now!* Reviewing the past, I may only rearrange my thoughts and feelings about an event. I feel the gift of the present moment.

Day 17

I am grateful that imagining the future, I direct my thoughts and feelings about what might be my highest and best desire. In this moment, I live within God and feel that all is well.

Day 18

I am grateful that my home environment is pleasing, gracious and warm. All strangers are welcome and I feel the love that is being shared.

Day 19

I am grateful that all my basic needs are being met, and there are more resources in my life to share with others. I feel increasingly affluent.

Day 20

I am grateful that my creativity extends into many expressions, and I am continuing to learn new things every day. I feel the joy and value of this experience.

Day 21

I am grateful that there are no limitations on the places where my mind can take me. I am traveling the world in my spirited imagination. I am feeling relaxed and free!

December

I am grateful that in this moment, I feel filled with God's presence and more completely accept that it is the joy of the One that energizes and *is* my life. Once more there is another opportunity for me to return from the far country of hesitation or doubt, into the sunshine of eternal life, united with the Infinite.

Whatever my current path of understanding, there is the siren song, the mystic melody enticing me to return to *my center* within God. Every return is greeted with a reconnection, the loving open arms and *voice of God* whispering, "Welcome home dear one! All is well with you!" I have a deep-felt gratitude for knowing this Truth and for accepting the gift of God's presence in my life.

My Personal Gratitude Affirmations

Day 22

I am grateful that music is in my life. It enriches, stimulates, celebrates, soothes, creates and brings joyous feelings to my heart.

Day 23

I am grateful that every day in every way, there are new possibilities for exploration and learning. I am feeling very enriched!

Day 24

I am grateful that I am living in such a time as this, with rapidly expanding explorations to greater depths and into limitless space. It is a metaphor for all of life's opportunities. I am feeling adventurous!

Day 25

I am grateful that of all the gifts that may be given to me, love is the greatest, and my heart is filled with love. I feel increasingly peaceful.

Day 26

I am grateful that my life is rich with new challenges to expand and be empowered through spiritual study and the practical application of Truth principles. I am honored with all my opportunities.

Day 27

I am grateful that my family, extended family and friends are bearers of love and light. It is good! It is very good! I am feeling deeply thankful!

Day 28

I am grateful that I know, affirm and feel that "I am blessed!" every day, in so many diverse ways. I can feel the assurance deep within.

December

I am grateful that as this year is coming to a close, I take an inventory of my past accomplishments. There may have been times when I took an action or made a choice, and in hindsight marked it as a mistake. Each of those choices led me to my next level of understanding, and to new alternatives and possibilities.

From the unlimited God-view I am always my natural whole being that was originally created. Living within this potential for good, I celebrate each unfolding step along my life-path. In this precious, present moment, I renew my commitment to *BE* the most loving and intelligent expression of God that I can be, remembering that I live within God.

My Personal Gratitude Affirmations

_____
_____
_____
_____
_____
_____
_____
_____
_____
_____
_____
_____
_____
_____
_____
_____
_____
_____
_____
_____
_____

Day 29

I am grateful that the measurement of a person's life is by the love and compassion that they have shared with others. I am feeling blessed as *I* share.

Day 30

I am grateful that the grace of God is eternally acting in my life, and I am always assured that the Source is the origin of my joy.

Day 31

I am grateful I know that circumstances usually change. The *unchanging* love of God, and the power of the law "it is done unto you *as* you believe," is a solid foundation from which to live. Something new and exciting is appearing in my life, and I embrace this experience *now!*

About the author

Clancy Blakemore is an ordained minister, counselor and educator with many years experience as a transformation facilitator for spiritual and personal growth. Semi-retired, she continues her work with people of all ages.

- Masters Degree in Education, University of La Verne
- Ph.D in Psychology, Lyon International University
- D.D. United Church of Religious Science

Clancy lives with her husband Richard near Sequoia National Park, in California. She said, "We have many fourth cousins we haven't met yet. Our door is open and all are welcome!"

clancy@clancyblakemore.com

CPSIA information can be obtained at www.ICGtesting.com
Printed in the USA
BVOW030712161012

303056BV00001BA/1/P